Foreword

$\mathcal{F}$or some visitors the sight of heritage steam locomotives thundering along the Nene Valley Railway is a delightful trip down memory lane. For many more the sights, sounds and smells of the golden age of steam are an exciting new experience as they take a trip back in time. Whether we evoke memories of days gone by or bring the past to life for new generations, the members of the Nene Valley Railway are proud to ensure that some of our city's heritage has been maintained and preserved for everyone to enjoy.

Since its official opening to the public in 1977, the Nene Valley Railway has developed and grown, thanks to the dedicated volunteers who devote so much of their time and energy to the Railway. New members are always welcome and opportunities are available to Bec Rail travel concessions and regular copies of our magazine *Nene Steam* which will keep you in touch with our activities and progress. Application forms are available from the Wansford Station Booking Office or you can write to us here at Wansford Station, Stibbington, Peterborough PE8 6LR.

On behalf of all members, I hope that you have a very enjoyable visit and that you will tell all your friends about the Nene Valley Railway where it's full steam ahead for a great day out!

Martin Sixsmith

Chairman
Nene Valley Railway

LNER A4 4-6-2 'Sir Nigel Gresley' gets the right away to depart Orton Mere.

LMS Black 5 4-6-0 No. M 5337 storms out of Wansford Tunnel with a Yarwell bound train.

Arriving at Wansford LNER J-27 No. 65894 crosses the River Nene swollen by the Easter floods in 1998.

Front Cover Picture:
Newly restored 'Battle of Britain' Class 4-6-2 No. 34081 '92 Squadron' makes an impressive sight departing Peterborough Nene Valley on its first weekend in traffic.   Photo: Paul Bason

Back Cover Picture:
The Nene Valley's maid of all work Austerity 0-6-0ST No. 75006 heads towards Yarwell.
Photo: Paul Bason

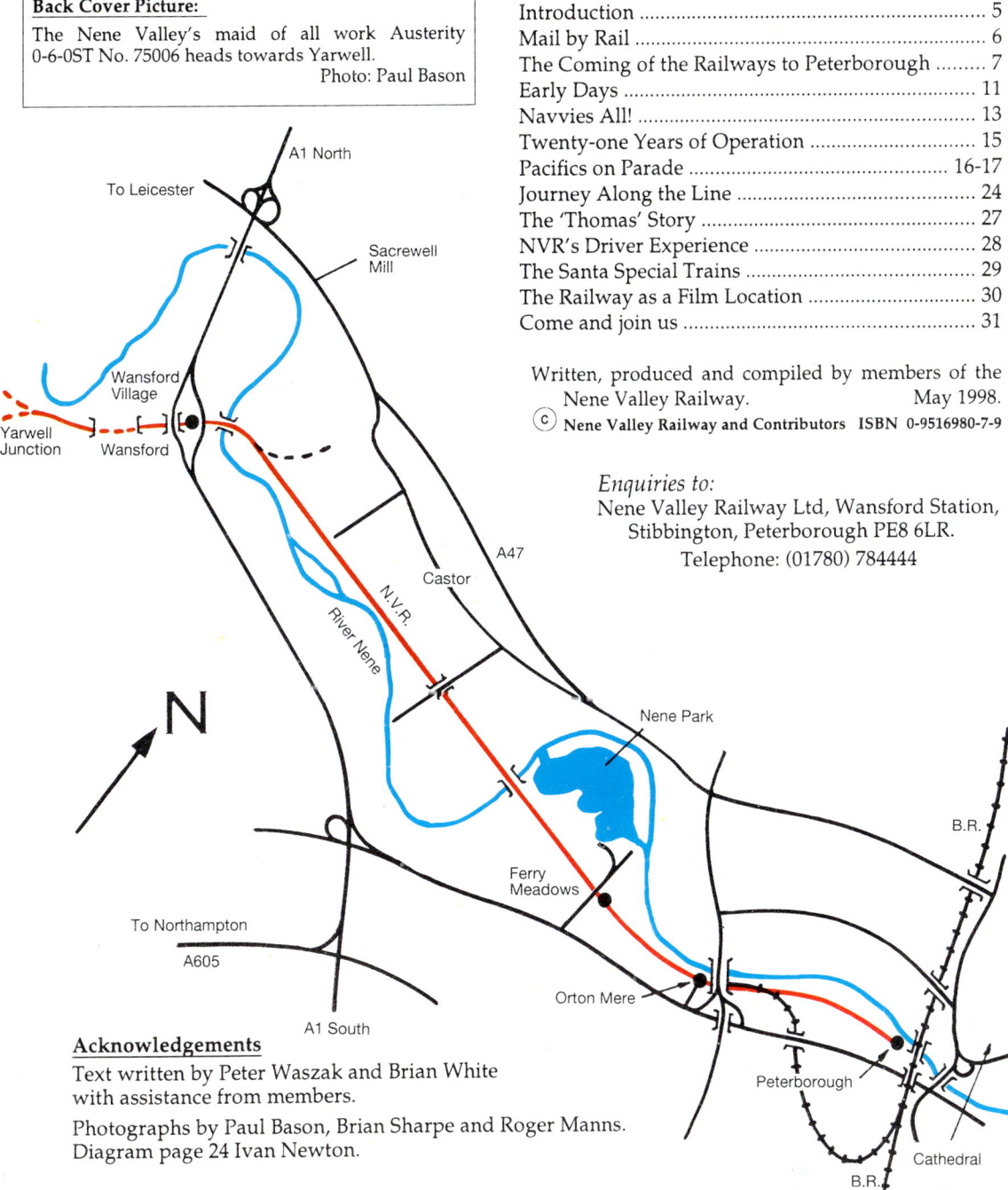

Contents

Foreword 3
Introduction 5
Mail by Rail 6
The Coming of the Railways to Peterborough 7
Early Days 11
Navvies All! 13
Twenty-one Years of Operation 15
Pacifics on Parade 16-17
Journey Along the Line 24
The 'Thomas' Story 27
NVR's Driver Experience 28
The Santa Special Trains 29
The Railway as a Film Location 30
Come and join us 31

Written, produced and compiled by members of the Nene Valley Railway.   May 1998.
© Nene Valley Railway and Contributors ISBN 0-9516980-7-9

Enquiries to:
Nene Valley Railway Ltd, Wansford Station, Stibbington, Peterborough PE8 6LR.
Telephone: (01780) 784444

Acknowledgements
Text written by Peter Waszak and Brian White with assistance from members.

Photographs by Paul Bason, Brian Sharpe and Roger Manns. Diagram page 24 Ivan Newton.

Printed by Starprint, Highlode Industrial Estate, Ramsey, Cambs. Tel: (01487) 710977
Typesetting: A. E. Sugars, Ramsey St. Mary's Cambs. Tel: (01733) 844412
Reproduction by Leicester Photo Litho. Tel: 0116 254 4101

NENE VALLEY RAILWAY
VISITORS GUIDE

£2.50

Introduction

The NVR is a standard gauge railway which runs for seven and a half miles between Yarwell Junction and Peterborough in Cambridgeshire. Its headquarters are at Wansford beside the A1, the old Great North Road, and are easily accessible from a large part of the country. The NVR is unique; nowhere in Britain or Europe is there a steam railway which can boast of locomotives and rolling stock from eleven different countries.

The railway is a family attraction, is the home of 'Thomas' the children's favourite engine and an educational charity which aims to bring back memories to those who knew, or to introduce to those who are too young, the experience of railway travel of the past, particularly in the days of steam.

The NVR operates for the benefit of day trippers, tourists and enthusiasts. Services operate at weekends from March to October with more frequent services on certain weekdays in the mid summer and including School Specials during June. A diesel multiple unit service is operated at off-peak times.

The standard ticket is a Day Rover ticket, allowing unlimited travel, one complete journey taking 85 minutes. The railway holds special events including 'Thomas Days', 'Vintage Weekends', 'Enthusiasts' Weekends' and the Christmas 'Santa Special' trains.

Full visitor facilities including toilets, baby changing facilities, refreshments, a bar and giftshop where souvenirs may be purchased, are available at Wansford as well as a museum and model railway. Particular attention is given to the needs of the elderly and handicapped, any difficulties being willingly dealt with by members of staff upon request. Wansford now boasts full ramped access to all platforms, ramps to trains and a modern disabled toilet in the new purpose-built visitor amenity/station building. Limited facilities are also available at stations along the line. Bar services are available on most trains with a Restaurant Car facility available for the larger pre-booked party. Car parking is available at Wansford and near other Nene Valley Railway stations.

Peterborough Nene Valley Station is to the south of the city centre and is within easy walking distance of the main line railway station and bus station via the Rivergate Shopping precinct.

A flexible charter service is available to private and corporate clients, including dining facilities on the beautiful Wagon Lits restaurant car together with the new corporate hospitality Wagon Lits salon. These services are also available on non-scheduled service days.

A young visitor admires ex-London Transport Sentinel diesel No. DL83.

Mail by Rail

The Nene Valley Railway has always had strong links with Post Office services since its inception in 1845. As a heritage railway this association has continued to the present day with three aspects of rail/mail activity.

Railway Letter Service: The RLS was first introduced in 1891 under an agreement between the Postmaster General and 75 railway companies to send mail to places accessible by rail but ill-served by the General Post Office; letters had to bear a normal postage stamp *in addition* to the stamp provided by the particular railway.

The service operates today, still under an agreement with Royal Mail, and visitors may send a letter by the RLS during a visit. Some superb special commemorative covers and special RLS stamps are available.

Travelling Post Office: The NVR has TWO Travelling Post Offices (TPO), one an ex-Southern Railway coach on loan from the National Railway Museum (NRM) which houses the railway's museum exhibition, the other vehicle the subject of an ambitious project to fully restore the only surviving TPO coach from the infamous Great Train Robbery of 1963. This TPO has a working apparatus system and will one day allow demonstrations to take place along the line. The TPO project is supported by a "Friends" scheme and anyone interested should ask for details.

'Postie Pete': is a familiar sight at many of the NVR's special events in his beautifully restored Morris van. 'Pete' gives demonstrations of despatching mails on to the train and then nips along to another station where he removes his mail. On theme-type events this really gives a flavour of rural lines in the heyday of British railways and also demonstrates the co-operation between Royal Mail, Peterborough, who own the van, and where 'Pete' is a postal official.

Bottom: Travelling Post Office Coach No. M30272M.
Below: Vintage Post Office Van.
Right: Railway Letter Service cover.

The Coming of the Railways to Peterborough

An early view of Wansford Station.

The first railway to arrive in Peterborough came from Blisworth, via Northampton, Thrapston, Oundle and Wansford with the very first passenger train along the Nene Valley departing Peterborough at 7 o'clock on Monday morning 2nd June, 1845. The Nene Valley Railway of today is the eastern section of this line. Being the first railway to reach the city it gave a connection to London (Euston). This was a branch of the railway which constructed the London to Birmingham main line (opened in May 1838). The branch was known as the Blisworth, Northampton & Peterborough Railway, sanctioned by an Act of Parliament in 1843 and which, in 1846, was incorporated into part of the London & North Western Railway Company.

A crowd of over 8,000 people welcomed the train to Peterborough, and that was when Peterborough's population was under 7,000. They filled the Fair Meadow and the station close to London Road. Church bells rang. Bands played, and the railway passengers went off to inns, a waxworks exhibition, a theatre and the Market Place.

According to the *Stamford Mercury*, at 4 o'clock a second train from London arrived causing *"extreme mortification, confusion and unpleasantness"*. Passengers from the first train (they should have left an hour previously) filled the second. Passengers from the second went to buy tickets home – then found the train full. More carriages were found and filled. People packed the carriage roofs. Two men fought with sticks (then, because they were endangering women and children, adjourned the fight until the journey's end). Many were left behind.

When the train eventually left it was so overcrowded, with large numbers standing on the carriage roofs, that the guard had to stop the train before the Lynch and Castor road-over bridges to order people to 'duck' before the train could proceed! The *Stamford Mercury* said, *"it was gratifying everything had passed off so pleasantly"*.

Steaming at a sedate pace towards Peterborough an early train is hauled by the Locomotion replica during the Peterborough 150 celebrations in 1995.

The Railway was now in operation but it had been a near thing. At a meeting in Thrapston powerful land-owners lined up against the intruder. The meeting was attended by the Earl Fitzwilliam of Milton Estates, part of which the present line crosses over. The good Earl argued that the proposal was *"manifestly absurd"*, and was supported by Lord Lilford and Lord Carysfoot of Elton. On the other hand, the Bishop of Peterborough gave considerable support to the enterprise along with the Duke of Cleveland.

An anonymous poet waxing lyrical about the widespread social changes the new railway would bring wrote:

"You will ride up to London in three hours and a quarter

With nothing to drive you but a kettle of hot water".

adding:

"No drunken stagecoachmen to break peoples necks".

and noting:

"that redundant horses would be converted if possible into pork lard".

The new railway followed an 'easy' route along the lush water meadows of the River Nene, engineered by Robert Stephenson and George Bidder costing £429,409 (about £9,000 a mile), a remarkably low figure for that period, and taking little more than a year to build.

Wansford tunnel (617 yards) and the nearby bridges over the River Nene were major undertakings, and by summer 1844 1,000 men were working on them. Many of the men and some of their wives lived in earth huts sometimes demolished by wind or quarrels. Labourers were paid 12 shillings a week, tunnel men 30 shillings. Accidents were frequent, and a doctor was

Wansford Station track layout 1877.

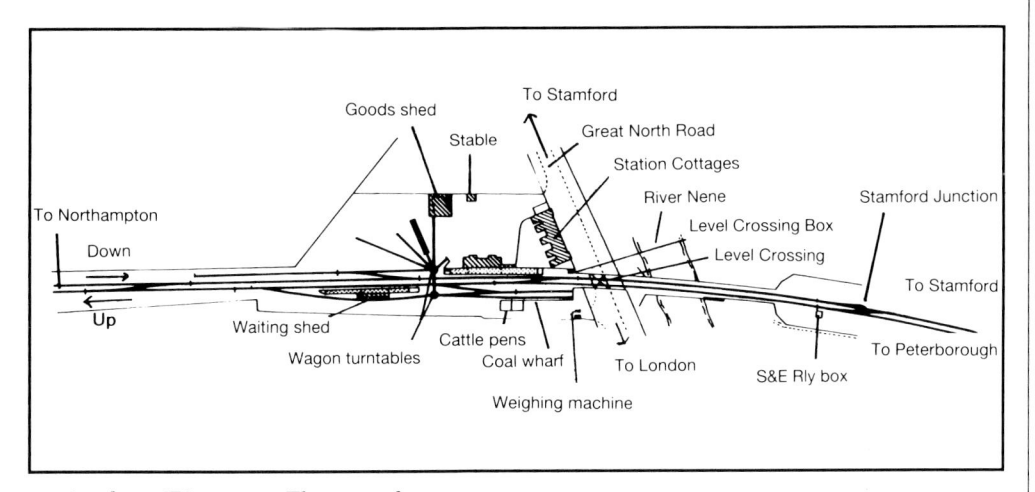

retained at £70 a year. The tunnel was cut from stone and soil, propped with wood, then lined with bricks baked from Sibson and Yarwell clay.

Instances of rowdyism and fighting occurred frequently and as a result two police officers from Manchester were despatched to Wansford to keep the peace. In Peterborough the local authorities, fearing the *"influx of bad characters"* strengthened the city police force from four to five men!

The railway's first timetable showed five trains each way each day except Sundays, when there were two each way. The fastest Peterborough-Northampton train took one and three quarter hours for the 42½ miles. London (Euston) was reached three hours later. The third class Peterborough – Northampton fare was 3s 7d and the third class Peterborough-London fare 17s.

At first only a single track had been laid, running on stone sleepers (examples of which are on display at Wansford), though bridges and tunnels were wide enough for two. Trains left Peterborough and Blisworth at the same time and passed at Thrapston. Within months traffic was so heavy a second track was needed. It was in use by the end of 1846 – the year that the Blisworth, Northampton Railway became part of the London & North Western Railway (LNWR).

This line was one of the first in the country to be equipped with electric telegraph apparatus being included from the inception. Despite the initial cost it resulted in numerous operating advantages.

By now 'railway mania' had the country in its grip with George 'King' Hudson at its head. He aimed to extend the Midland Counties Railway to Peterborough and on into the Fens via his Eastern Counties Railway ahead of a rival line from London. The Syston and Peterborough Railway (Syston was a junction off the Leicester to Derby line of the MC Railway) was constructed in three sections, the Stamford to Peterborough section opening on 2nd September, 1846. Closely following this the Eastern Counties Railway from Ely via March arrived in Peterborough 10 months ahead of the contract date, opening to passengers on 14th January, 1847. At this point Peterborough became a 'through' station, it now being possible to reach London via two directions. However, the direct route from London was now approaching the city.

The missing link of the Midland Counties line was completed on the 1st May, 1848. The next to arrive was the Great Northern Railway from Doncaster via Lincoln and Boston to Werrington Junction opened on

17th October, 1848. The GNR line from the south opened on 5th October, 1850. Two years later the line was extended on 15th July, 1852 via Helpston, Tallington and Grantham to Retford (Towns Line).

Peterborough's second link with East Anglia and the last major line to arrive was what became the Midland & Great Northern Joint which opened on 1st August, 1866.

Three further openings had a direct influence on the Nene Valley line. In 1867 Wansford became a junction with the opening of the Sibson Extension (Wansford Branch) of the Stamford & Essendine Railway. The single tracked line joined the LNWR 80 yards east of Wansford station and survived until 1st June, 1929.

Before the 1870s, cross-country travel from Peterborough was a tortuous journey along the Northampton line towards Birmingham, requiring a change of direction at Blisworth making the LNWR route considerably longer than the competing Midland route via Leicester. On 1st November, 1879 the LNWR opened its 11 mile connecting line from Yarwell Junction (to the west of Wansford) to Seaton on the Rugby and Stamford Railway, also part of the LNWR network. The Peterborough to Rugby line was then developed as a secondary main line, linking Yarmouth to Birmingham and Peterborough to North Wales and Ireland.

The third connecting line was the one and three quarter mile Fletton Loop opened in 1883. The loop, from the Great Northern main line at Fletton Junction to the Nene Valley line at Longville Junction, enabled Great Northern trains to run from Peterborough North to Leicester (Belgrave Road) via Rockingham, Medbourne and Lowesby Junction, which system also gave access to Market Harborough and Melton Mowbray.

Passenger services (sometimes hauled by Patrick Stirling's famous 2-2-2 locomotives which had one pair of eight feet diameter driving wheels) ended in 1916, but sugar beet traffic continued until February 1991. Longville Junction was taken out in 1929, reinstated in 1947, taken out about 1961 and reinstated again in 1974 to give the new Nene Valley Railway a connection to British Rail.

The LNWR ran Peterborough-Rugby and Peterborough-Northampton trains along the valley until the 1923 grouping took the line into the London Midland & Scottish Railway (LMS).

In 1948 the railways were nationalised but changes were few at first. However, in the 1950s and 1960s came the period of rationalisation. Traffic and services declined as passengers took to car and coach and goods were increasingly conveyed by lorry. Stations closed, Orton in 1942 and Castor and Wansford in 1957. Locomotives became run-down and dirty. Passenger trains between Peterborough and Northampton ceased on 2nd May, 1964 and there was no freight beyond Oundle from this date. Wansford goods facilities were withdrawn on 13th July, 1964. On the Rugby line, the passenger service ended on 6th June, 1966, just one week after the introduction of an improved electrified service at Rugby to Crewe and the north.

The Nene Valley line's main surviving traffic was ironstone from Nassington Quarries to the west of Wansford. This service ceased in 1971. The thrice weekly goods service to Oundle and the occasional 'Oundle School Special' ceased in 1972. In that year British Rail closed the line completely with the one hundred and twenty-seven years' story at an end. One chapter in the line's history had now closed but another was about to begin.

Early Days

In 1955 Richard Paten an engineer, who later became a local clergyman, visited North America and was impressed by the number of towns which had placed old redundant steam locomotives on plinths in order to commemorate the vital contribution the railway made to the growth of a particular town. Rev Paten was determined to do the same for Peterborough and in 1968 just after the end of steam on British Rail he purchased BR Class '5' 4-6-0 No 73050 for £3,000, its scrap value, with the intention of displaying it on a plinth outside the local Technical College. Although BR had officially banned steam from its network the locomotive travelled under its own power from Patricroft, Manchester to New England locomotive shed in Peterborough under cover of darkness! Its arrival on 11th September, 1968 generated considerable local interest. Because the locomotive was found to be in good condition there was resistance to the idea that 73050 should be 'stuffed' – rather it should be restored to full working order. With the closure of New England shed the engine moved in September 1968 to a temporary storage compound at Peterborough East.

On 28th March, 1969 the Peterborough branch of the East Anglia Locomotive Preservation Society was established by 16 members. The initial aim of the society had been to purchase and restore the BR Pacific No. 70000 'Britannia'. Because of their similar aims the society was now able to welcome the Peterborough group into their midst. After various negotiations 73050 moved to a more permanent home at the rail-connected Westwood Sidings of Baker Perkins Ltd where volunteers commenced restoration work. By February 1970 the local branch with fifty members, was sufficiently strong to form their own association, the Peterborough Locomotive Society.

BR Class 5MT No. 73050 and Hunslet 0-6-0ST 'Jacks Green' at an Open Day at the British Sugar Factory.

Hudswell Clarke 0-6-0ST 'Derek Crouch' arrives at Wansford in 1974.

11

The following year BR were about to remove the rail connection at Westwood and 73050 was moved to a new home at the British Sugar Corporation's Peterborough factory sidings, where it was joined by a Hunslet 0-6-0 locomotive 'Jack's Green', which had arrived under its own steam when the local Nassington Ironstone Quarry closed. The PLS held its first Public Open Day during Easter 1970 and its first steam day with 'Jack's Green a year later!

In the meantime important events were taking place on a broader front. In 1970 the Government's plan to relocate the old Clapham Transport Museum to York prompted the PLS to join forces with Peterborough Development Corporation – the City was now a 'New Town' the population of which would double in 15 years. The City Council and the County Council submitted a detailed proposal to set up a National Transport Museum based around the old Peterborough East Station, which it was suggested should be run in conjunction with a preserved steam railway along the Nene Valley line.

Although it is still regretted that this imaginative proposal was rejected, it was clear that there was local support for a steam railway along the Nene Valley. In January 1972 in line with its wider interests the PLS changed its name to the Peterborough Railway Society and in March held a well attended Public Meeting at the Town Hall at which the idea of the Nene Valley Railway was formally launched.

PRS officers co-operated with the Development Corporation, City and County Councils in the production of a feasibility report which was published in June 1972. It supported the establishment of a steam railway through the heart of the future 2,000 acre Nene Park, which was to be developed as the leisure centrepiece of the new Greater Peterborough. With the announcement that BR was to close the surviving portion of the Northampton line, the PRS organised a last train to Oundle which ran on November 4th, 1972; the line then officially closed.

In March 1974 the Peterborough Development Corporation bought the Nene Valley line between Longville and Yarwell Junctions and leased it to the PRS to operate the railway – a major milestone in the society's history.

BR Class 5MT No. 73050 'City of Peterborough' pauses at a Wansford Open Day in 1975.

Navvies All!

Nord compound 4-6-0 No. 3.628 storms away from Wansford.

Visitors often ask "Why all the foreign locomotives and carriages? Why did the NVR go Continental?" The answer is part planning and part chance. In 1974 the task then facing society volunteers was enormous. Knowing that the line was to close BR had neglected maintenance. Most of the stations had been demolished with Wansford station and yard sold into private use. There was no connection with BR or to the British Sugar Corporation factory where the society's stock was kept, no passing loop and only a head-shunt for a siding. Wansford station had just one short low platform and chickens had been kept in the signal-box. The stations at Ferry Meadows and Orton Mere did not exist. The line had virtually to be rebuilt from scratch.

The initial idea was to use former BR locomotives and stock. However, as the NVR arrived late on the scene, the only passenger locomotives available were rusting hulks from Barry Scrapyard in South Wales, the restoration of which would be a long and costly process. Further, at the time surplus BR carriage stock was in short supply. The PDC who had paid out a considerable sum of money were anxious that passenger services should commence as soon as possible and certainly before the opening of the Nene Park in 1978. The society which by then had one main line locomotive and several small ex-industrial locomotives, which were unsuitable to operate a service over a 5½ miles line, faced a major problem.

In 1973 PRS member Richard Hurlock had approached the Society about providing a home for his ex-Swedish Railways 2-6-4T Class S1 oil-fired No 1928. This locomotive arrived at the BSC sidings in March 1974. Because of its dimensions, a little higher and wider than British stock, the engine was to be a static exhibit only. During 1974 it was slowly realised that the use of foreign locomotives, particularly those which had come out of strategic reserve and would be in excellent condition, might be an answer to NVR's prayers.

Could the Nene Valley Railway loading gauge be extended to the International Transit or 'Berne' loading gauge? If so, the Nene Valley Railway would offer the unique spectacle of British and Continental locomotives and stock running alongside one another in Britain.

Following examination our Civil Engineer concluded that a single bridge demolition plus platform alterations at Wansford would allow operation to Continental loading gauge. Railway Inspectorate approval, subject to certain provisions to speed and clearances followed in 1974. The decision to operate to Berne gauge was made.

In April 1973 British Rail gave the PRS permission to use Wansford signal-box as its new Wansford base which allowed the restoration process to commence. In September the first items of stock arrived including a 'shoc' van body as a store, a Planet 4 wheeled petrol locomotive and some trollies, which enabled the railway to operate its first works train. On 3rd November, 1973 a Tenancy Agreement was signed with BR for the Wansford site excluding the old station building and yard which had been sold into private use.

However, before stock could be moved from the BSC base, the missing section of the Fletton Loop towards Longville Junction had to be relaid. Following the laying of 1,200 feet of track in March 1974, a special train was run to Wansford hauled by 'Derek Crouch' for PRS, Peterborough Development Corporation and City Council officials. Stock was then moved to Wansford for the Easter weekend, when for the first time 'Wansford Steam Centre' opened to the public. A steam shuttle service through the tunnel to Yarwell did not start until the following year.

Between 1974 and May 1977 upgrading of the line to passenger standards meant a great deal of work. At Wansford the original platplatform was extended, the second track re-laid across Wansford bridge over the River Nene and linked up to track through the future platform 2, signals erected and points re-connected and the signal-box returned to an operational state. Further land to the south of the railway was acquired for loco yard sidings and future shed, and for public car parking. Coal and water facilities for the locomotives were also provided. Although the Society had hoped to use the original station building and platform, this did not prove possible and in 1977 the old wooden station building from Barnwell was acquired and transported to Wansford by road where Manpower Services Commission labour helped to erect it on platform 2. At the Peterborough end during the summer of 1976 a run-round loop was installed at what became Orton Mere station and a start made on platform construction.

Other vital tasks involved the recruitment and training of volunteer staff for footplate and operating duties, remedial work to make safe the east portal of Wansford tunnel and the provision of visitor facilities for toilets and refreshments. The demolition of the low Lynch Bridge in January 1976 enabled all the continental locomotives to be moved to Wansford. Further locomotives arrived including a Danish F Class 0-6-0T and the French Nord express passenger engine. Particularly welcome was the Southern Electric Group's rake of ex-Southern air-braked carriages which could be used with the railway's air-braked foreign locomotives. British stock also arrived including the 'Battle of Britain' light Pacific No 34081 from Barry Scrapyard and some ex-BR Mk 1 carriages.

On 1st January, 1977 the first General Manager was appointed charged with the day-to-day running of the railway, to promote the railway and to oversee its commercial operations.

On 24th May Major Rose, the Railway Inspector, inspected and passed the railway as fit for passenger carrying operations. Following the granting of a Light Railway Order, the line between Wansford and Orton Mere was officially opened on 1st June, public services commencing on 4th June. The first train was hauled by the 'Nord' and Swedish No 1178 and used the SEG carriages.

14

Twenty One Years of Operation – and moving to the Millennium

Once the euphoria of opening had passed and the railway settled down into its operating routine, it was time to examine the way forward. Although the Railway was fortunate in taking over a line with most of the track intact and that work essential to reopening the line and running a passenger service had been completed, much was still to be done. Limitations of the track layout, platforms and signalling at Wansford and the short platform and absence of signalling at Orton Mere, placed serious limitations on operating flexibility. The Wansford-Yarwell section could not be used through lack of an additional track enabling the locomotive to pass from one end of the train to the other at Yarwell. With the arrival of further stock more siding space was required. Because of the lack of covered accommodation work on the locomotives and carriages had to be undertaken in the open – with obvious problems during the winter. Also, visitor facilities needed improving and Wansford station area required enhancement so that it was ready to welcome passengers.

During 1977 the increasing number of passengers made it obvious that on peak days, particularly Bank Holidays, a two train service would be required. In order to make this possible, over the winter of 1977-78 the original platform at Wansford (now platform 3) was both lengthened and raised to the correct height and an asphalt surface laid. In August 1978 a footbridge connecting both platforms was brought into use. To enable the operation of longer trains Orton Mere platform was extended to accommodate trains of six coaches in length.

With the Peterborough Development Corporation aiming to open their Nene Park during the summer of 1978, a single six coach platform was built at Ferry Meadows station, and a portable building acquired to provide station facilities. The station opened on 17th May. At Ham Lane, the old level crossing gates were replaced by an automatic crossing with lights.

The Nene Valley Railway's opening train passes Mill Lane on 1st June, 1077.

○ **PACIFICS**

LMS 4-6-2 No. 46229 'Duchess of Hamilton'

Centre: LNER 4-6-2 No. 60007 'Sir Nigel Gresley'

LNER 4-6-2 No. 60009 'Union of South Africa'

N PARADE

SR 4-6-2 No. 35005 'Canadian Pacific'

LNER 4-6-2 No. 60532 'Blue Peter'

Work began in April and the crossing was commissioned in August.

In September 1978 the 67 feet Wansford locomotive turntable was commissioned. This turntable originally of 60 feet diameter was built in 1933 by Ransomes & Rapier of Ipswich for Bourne station but in 1960 was removed to Peterborough East station.

When the line was opened in 1977 the eastern terminus was at Orton Mere although a track continued past Longville Junction and the Fletton Loop, still used by BR for seasonal sugar beet traffic, to join the East Coast Main Line at Fletton Junction. Orton Mere, two miles by road from the city centre was not a natural terminus. Visitors arriving in the city by public transport and knowing nothing about local bus services were finding it difficult to find Orton Mere. Other railways with a BR connection were receiving charter trains. For the NVR the obvious answer was for BR to run a shuttle service between Peterborough and Orton Mere. At this time BR were upgrading the Fletton Loop in preparation for modern high capacity wagons being used on the BSC traffic. In effect the line was being upgraded to passenger standards free of charge! However, the NVR had still to improve the section of line between the BSC sidings and Longville Junction laid by Society members in 1974.

In 1974 a redundant ex-Midland Railway signal-box had been obtained from Maxey Road crossing Helpston and brought by road to the future Orton Mere station site. In 1976 the foundations were constructed for the box although in the short term a ground frame was in operation. In 1978 a 12-lever frame from Nene Junction signal-box was installed complete with signals and associated interlocking. The box was designed so that it could be locked out of use when no signalman was on duty, but still permit trains to enter Orton Mere from Wansford. Following the signing of a Private Siding Agreement with BR, the railway-chartered BR shuttle service first ran at Eurosteam 1980 and was a success. Enthusiasts travelled long distances for the opportunity of travelling over a line which had not seen regular passenger services since 1916! BR ran a properly advertised service during high season, Sundays in 1981 but from 1982 to 1986 changed to Saturdays which offered better main line connections. With the opening of the Peterborough Extension, the service ceased in 1986 although the line can still be used by visiting charter trains and by NVR locomotives travelling to and from BR open days.

Southern Railway S15 4-6-0 No. 841 'Greene King' heads a visiting charter train.

With Orton Mere in operation, it was now possible to turn to reopening of the line to Yarwell. In 1980 the Railway Inspector had approved plans for Yarwell which involved re-laying 500 feet of track to the railway's western boundary and installing a 7 coach run-round loop, all to Berne clearances. Signalling alterations were also required at Wansford. In 1982 work was delayed by the James Bond film *Octopussy* which required the laying of a point in the centre of the tunnel! The Yarwell Extension finally opened for 'Eurosteam '83' on the 17th September. Swedish locomotive 1178 had the honour of working the first train. However, as yet no platform had been provided at Yarwell. From 1984 the main train service was extended through to Yarwell although on special occasions a shuttle service from Wansford operated.

In the meantime improvements were taking place at Wansford. In 1980 the first stage of the locomotive shed had been erected with associated working facilities. Steelwork for the 60 feet long two-road building had been obtained from the old Peterborough Pig Market. Phase two doubled the length of the shed. In 1983 film revenue from *Octopussy* paid for a single road carriage and wagon shed, new access being provided from a point west of the A1 road bridge. Platform 3 was also extended.

The major project of the first decade was the Peterborough Extension. When the Peterborough Development Corporation opened negotiations with BR for the purchase of the line, BR agreed to sell the Wansford-Longville Junction section for a price which reflected agricultural land values. However, for the Peterborough-Longville Junction section BR demanded a price which related to the industrial development prices. As the PDC declined to accept the latter, the NVR terminated at Orton Mere. In 1975 BR removed the track east of Longville Junction leaving the land derelict. By the early 1980s as BR had still failed to sell the track-bed for industrial development (the main stumbling block being lack of road access) negotiations reopened with the PDC for the disposal of the land and agreement was soon reached. The way was now clear for the NVR to revive earlier proposals of operating to Peterborough.

Following the go ahead for the 1½ miles extension from the NVR Council, outline planning permission was obtained by the end of 1983. On May 2nd, 1984 at a ceremony at Longville Junction an Extension Appeal was launched. In September track

Swedish 2-6-2T No. 1178 and Peckett 0-6-0ST No. 2000 with a mixed goods train during Eurosteam 1983.

French Compound 4-6-0 No. 3.628 nears Castor with a train of Danish coaches.

LMS Black Five No. 44767 'George Stephenson' arrives at Wansford.

The NVR's flagship locomotive BR 4-6-0 No. 73050 'City of Peterborough' heads away from Wansford.

laying commenced from Longville Junction working east but by the end of the year track laying took place at Peterborough working westwards, link-up being achieved the following year. At Peterborough, Manpower Services Commission labour was used to construct the seven coach platform. At Longville Junction the Fletton Loop track was severed and a second track laid to Orton Mere which enabled Orton Mere signal-box to control both the Peterborough NVR and the NVR end of the BR Fletton Loop line. Following a Department of Transport inspection the first passenger train ran to Peterborough Nene Valley on Saturday, 24th May, 1986 hauled by Swedish 4-6-0 No 101.

In February 1985 HRH Prince Edward, then a student at Cambridge University, unofficially visited the railway as part of his promotion of the University Rag Week which involved being tied to the track in front of a locomotive! After the photographs had been taken, Neil Vann, the then Chairman, took the opportunity of inviting the Prince to return and open the extension the following summer.

The Prince readily agreed and did so on June 30th, 1986. After a tour of Wansford, the Prince joined 73050 'City of Peterborough' and drove it under supervision to Peterborough. Prince Edward accepted Honorary Life Membership of the NVR and so is able to keep in touch with developments.

Following the opening of the Peterborough Extension it was time again to turn to less glamorous but no less vital tasks. A four road locomotive storage shed has been added south of the existing shed, the steelwork having been obtained from redundant London Brick Company drying sheds. At last the majority of the NVR locomotive fleet could be kept under cover. The erection of the steelwork was one of the last tasks achieved by unemployed people from the Manpower

Services Commission and Youth Training programmes. With the introduction of Employment Training, the NVR has no longer been offered a similar source of labour.

In order to make better use of the Yarwell Extension and to increase operating flexibility through Wansford station in 1987 a new cross-over was installed west of the A1 road bridge. This involved extensive changes to the interlocking of Wansford signal-box. Because of the distance to the signal-box the new cross-over has point motors and track circuiting, the first on the NVR.

In July 1987 a locomotive water tank was obtained ex- London Transport, Barking, which has since been erected at Peterborough Nene Valley station. In 1990 four Belgian carriages arrived, a 1st/3rd composite, a high capacity 98-seater and two 1st class carriages.

During September 1993 the Wansford loco yard was re-laid enabling easier loading and unloading of locomotives from road transport. The new yard also gave extra siding spacing and more manouevrability for the locomotives as well as an opportunity for additional platform space adjacent the new Wansford Station building. This was completed in 1995 during a season of special events celebrating the 150th Anniversary of the coming of railways to Peterborough.

Although a building contractor was employed to construct Wansford's showpiece station/visitor amenity building to a traditional design, the NVR's volunteer gangs also played a vital role building the Buffet Platform extension in 1996, Platform 2 extension in 1997 and, after the erection of an impressive signal gantry adjacent to the level crossing in 1998, the completion of a new canopy over the platform next to the Gift Shop.

In the spring of 1998 the NVR once again hosted commercial freight traffic in the form of 900 tonne pipe trains from Scotland. Arriving via the Fletton Loop NVR motive power in the form of a Class 14 diesel took over at Orton Mere for the last leg of the journey to Yarwell. Completed just in time for the NVR's 21st Birthday later in the same year, the Battle of Britain Locomotive Society's impressive Pacific No. 34081 '92 Squadron' entered NVR service after a mammoth 21-year restoration to full working order, a credit indeed to all those involved.

The new signal gantry and station building at Wansford make an ideal frame for J-27 No. 65894.

SR 4-6-2 No. 35005 Canadian Pacific prepares to leave Peterborough.

Class 40 diesel No. D306 in charge of a demonstration freight train at Longueville Junction.

Journey Along the Line

Most passengers join at Wansford which is a through station. The train usually departs to the west, passes under the A1 and runs through a steep cutting before entering Wansford tunnel, which is 617 yards in length. The tunnel is straight and level and has no ventilation shafts. At the far end the line curves gently south until it emerges from a wooded cutting to terminate at Yarwell Junction on an embankment south of the River Nene and between the Sibson Trout Fisheries. From this point following the run round of the engine, the train makes its way to Peterborough Nene Valley Station.

After returning to Wansford the train leaves, crossing the Old Great North Road by a level crossing at the eastern end of the station. During peak traffic times before the dual carriageway bypass was constructed in 1959 this crossing was a major bottleneck and on summer Saturdays the gates were sometimes shut against road traffic for up to 20 minutes at a time. The signals at the platform ends are two of the few surviving Great Northern Railway somersault signals, once a familiar sight to passengers along the East coast main line.

On the north side of the line, sandwiched between the road and the river is Wansford signal-box, one of the largest preserved operational boxes in Britain. It was built in 1907 and its 60-lever frame replaced three earlier signal-boxes. The signalman also controls the level crossing gates.

The railway crosses the River Nene on a girder bridge followed by a series of brick arches over the river flood plain and passes the site of the junction with the Stamford branch. This line was closed in 1929 but the course of the railway can easily be followed as the overgrown embankment curves north towards the village of Sutton. Despite being over 60 years since the branch closed, all the intermediate stations are still in existence. The branch was opened in 1867 and its trains used a bay platform in the old Wansford station.

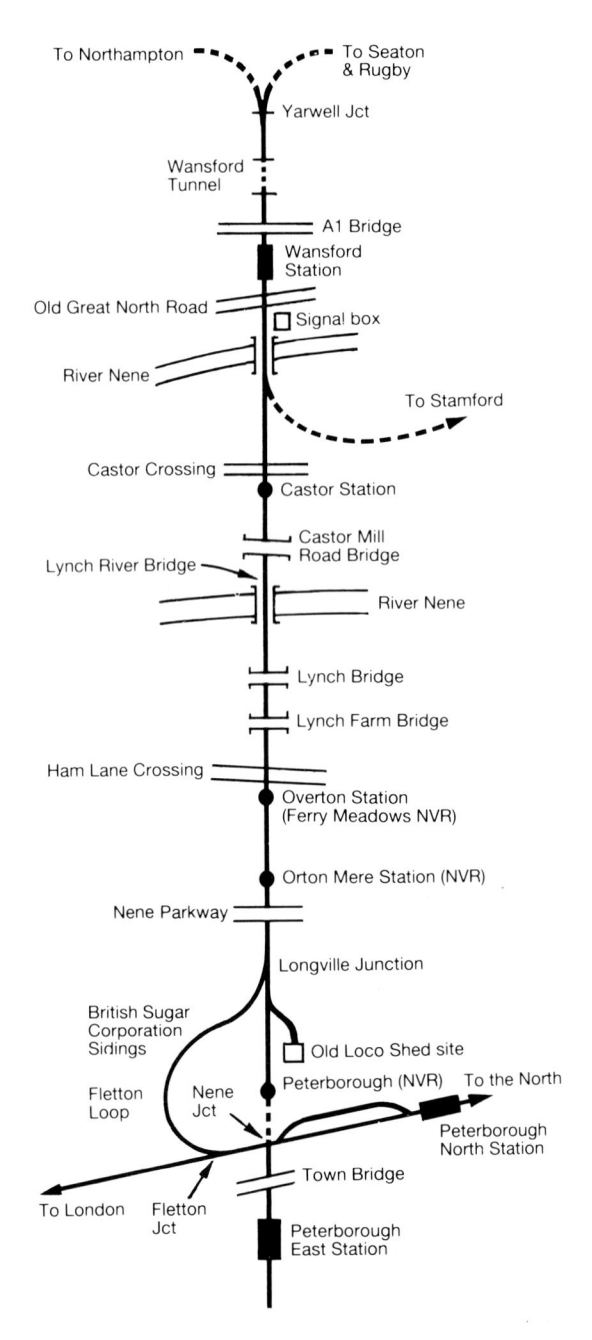

24

World famous LNER 4-6-2 No. 60103 'Flying Scotsman' leaves Wansford Tunnel with a train of restored vans.

Once across the river the Railway curves in an easterly direction for 400 yards on an embankment above the flood plain and then enters the long straight section of 3 miles to Ferry Meadows. This section of the Nene Valley is rich in history. To the south of the line across the fields can be seen the picturesque village of Water Newton. The water mill here was built in 1791.

Once over the Castor crossing the railway passes the site of Castor station, closed in 1957 and demolished soon after. The station was damaged by a 'doodle bug' flying bomb in the last war. Next we pass over Ermine Street, once a major Roman road, although nothing is now visible from ground level.

To the archaeologist this area is of great importance for it is the site of Durobrivae, centre of the Roman pottery industry. 'Castorware' was widely exported and has been found as far away as Turkey. Also from Durobrivae came the unique collection of early Christian silver plate, the Water Newton Treasure, now in the British Museum.

The railway continues past the twin villages of Ailsworth and Castor, in the distance to the north, where the tower of the Norman Church at Castor, dedicated to St. Kyneburgha, can be seen. Castor was also the site of one of the largest Roman villas found in Britain.

Beyond Castor the railway enters a shallow cutting, passes under Mill Road bridge and falls on a gradient of 1 in 270, the steepest on the line. Mill Road bridge is partially constructed from old stone blocks once used instead of timber sleepers when the London and Birmingham Railway was built in 1837. These blocks were also used to construct the façade of Wansford tunnel.

The railway crosses the River Nene for the second time on Lynch bridge. There is a speed restriction for trains over the bridge due to restricted clearances for continental rolling stock.

Over the river the railway enters Ferry Meadows Country Park, the centrepiece of the Nene Park Trust. In Ferry Meadows three lakes, covering 120 acres, were the result of gravel excavation. The largest of these, Overton Lake, can be seen to the north of the railway with Milton Ferry Bridge, built in 1716, in the distance.

The line now enters a wooded cutting and climbs gradually through Alwalton Lynch before descending gently to Ham Lane level crossing. Ham Lane was once just a farm access road but is now the main access to Ferry Meadows. To handle the extra traffic without undue delay the Railway installed a continental type crossing controlled by automatic flashing lights.

Over Ham Lane crossing is Ferry Meadows station, serving the central area of the Country Park. This is an excellent point for passengers to break their journey on the Nene Valley Railway to explore the park. Within a few hundred yards of the station are the park offices, information centre, snack bar and toilets. There is a large caravan and camping area, play areas for children as well as a miniature steam railway which runs from the information centre to Overton Lake sailing club.

Ferry Meadows is built on the site of Overton (later Orton Waterville) station which was closed in 1942.

Beyong Ferry Meadows the railway runs on an embankment between flood meadows, curving gradually to the north-east, passing the headquarters of the cruising club. After one mile it enters Orton Mere station which was built by the Railway partially under the bridge carrying Nene Parkway and has a good access from all parts of Peterborough. A footpath crosses the river at the locks known as Orton Staunch which gives access to Thorpe Wood golf course which is built over the site of a Roman fort covering 27 acres. As many as 2,500 soldiers were stationed here between 44 and 65 AD.

Soon after departing Orton Mere the main line link can be seen swinging away to the right at Longville Junction. The train passes the site of the British Sugar Corporation's Peterborough factory, closed in 1991. A mile further on the line runs alongside the river past Woodstone Staunch, once the site of the Co-op Wagon Works, closed in 1963.

As the train runs into Peterborough Nene Valley station, opened in 1986, it passes a signal-box which came from Welland Bridge in Spalding. The entire area between the station and the river was once the site of the London & North Western Railway Woodston Locomotive Sheds, which closed in 1932.

Various locomotives and rolling stock are stored in the yard at Peterborough, including some belonging to Railworld, an independent Museum of World Railways.

Passengers may break their journey at Peterborough and visit the City Centre which is only a short walk away along the riverside path and over one of two footbridges. The high level railway is the East Coast Main line while the lower level line is that of the Peterborough to East Anglia route. On the other hand for those who wish to make the return journey immediately there are various items of goods rolling stock for inspection.

The 'Thomas' Story

Although the Nene Valley Railway has bigger and more impressive steam engines, to most visitors and especially children, the Railway is the home of 'Thomas'. Certainly 'Thomas' is the NVR's most famous engine and one of the biggest attractions. Few of his friends, however, know how and why 'Thomas' received his name.

Hudswell Clarke engine 0-6-0T No 1800, built in 1947, spent all its working life at the British Sugar Corporation's Peterborough factory. By 1970 when the Peterborough Locomotive Society built its compound within the factory sidings, No 1800 was the regular stand-by locomotive. Thanks to its immaculate blue livery it soon became known as 'Thomas' to Society members. At the BSC National Sports and Family Day in 1971 and 1972 No 1800 was used to give people short brake van rides. In 1971 the Rev W Awdry, author of the 'Thomas' books came to one of the Open Days and agreed to name No 1800 'Thomas'.

In 1973 as 'Thomas' was in need of major repairs it was sold to the Peterborough Railway Society who stored it out of use until 1977 when parts of a similar locomotive were used to produce one good engine – 'Thomas'. By 1977 'Thomas' was back in action again.

In the past 'Thomas' has visited Didcot, Leicester and Cambridge promoting the Nene Valley Railway and has even switched on the Christmas lights in Peterborough! At Wansford he has attracted over 8,000 visitors during a single special weekend.

During 1990 to 1992 'Thomas' received a major overhaul costing in excess of £80,000 and now delights children of all ages.

The Rev. Awdry naming 'Thomas' in 1971.

NVR's Driving Experience

An eager enthusiast in the cab of '92 Squadron'

Ready for the off.

Since 'Flying Scotsman' visited the line in 1994 the Nene Valley Railway has offered budding footplate men and women the chance to enjoy the unique sensation of driving a full-sized steam locomotive. Accompanied by one of the NVR's experienced drivers, participants are given an insight into how a locomotive works, how it is driven, a visit to the yard and signal box and, of course, their own opportunity to take the controls. Everyone who takes part receives a personalised certificate, souvenirs of their visit and vouchers for a meal in the cafe and for membership of the railway.

The Nene Valley Driver Experience makes a memorable gift idea for birthdays, anniversaries and retirement surprises, what better way could there be to say 'thank you' to someone special.

Corporate Driver Experience events can be tailored to a Company's individual footplate and catering needs depending on numbers involved.

Unlike our normal services, advance booking is essential – for further details please call 01780 784444.

The Santa Special Trains

The Nene Valley Railway has run Santa Special trains for over 20 years and has carried over 330,000 passengers. These trains which run in December at weekends and on Wednesdays have developed a high reputation. It is not uncommon for visitors to travel long distances to ride on the NVR Santa Specials. Bookings have been received from people living on the south coast, London and the Home Counties, the West Midlands, Yorkshire and East Anglia. A booking has also been received from Washington DC! The NVR regularly receive coach parties from Leicester, Wellingborough, the Home Counties and Lincolnshire and these parties bring children from every section of the community. Santa trains have even been featured on Japanese Television!

Polish 2-10-0 No. 7173 in disguise as Santa at Mill Lane.

The first Santa Specials ran in 1977, the year the railway opened to Orton Mere, being the idea of the Railway's first General Manager. In that first season the NVR hoped to attract some 7,000 passengers but in fact nearly 10,000 bookings were received requiring a seven-coach train set when a maximum of four carriages had been considered adequate. In 1990 the NVR received some 25,500 bookings, ran 57 trains with up to 3,200 passengers on a single day.

Today with over 20,000 Santa visitors the operation must be planned with almost military precision, starting shortly after the New Year when the first of the following season's Santa presents are selected and ordered. Great care is taken to choose suitable presents with good value for money and play interest in mind. The presents begin to arrive in August when wrapping up to 13,000 presents commences. Bookings by post, 'phone and personal visit start in September. Nearer the time Santa's Grotto in the station building has to be erected, the train decorated and the required seasonal fayre ordered.

Santa meets the Driver.

29

The Railway as a Film Location

Between 1978 and 1998 well over 100 films, commercials and episodes for television have been made with the help of scenes shot on the Nene Valley Railway. Some have been major productions like *Octopussy* and *Dirty Dozen – Next Mission* while television companies have based episodes of series such as *Secret Army*, *Reilly Ace of Spies* and *Hannay* using the railway as an integral part of the plot. Commercial films have been set on or around the line often forming a distinctive backdrop, while current affairs programmes, pop groups, such as Queen, and railway orientated films have been made with impressive results.

The Nene Valley Railway lends itself naturally to filming by having a number of features which when combined provide a formidable bonanza of alternatives for film companies. The railway has a seven and a half miles length of track running over and alongside a river, traverses meadowland, cuttings, urban areas, passes an industrial complex and runs through a country park. The features like an imposing Victorian station building, a tunnel of over 600 yards and a manually operated four-gated level crossing controlled from a 60-lever signal-box all provide a diverse and historic appearance which is carefully nurtured by all concerned.

The locomotives and rolling stock are both British and foreign, providing a wide range of opportunity and subject matter for those whose business is film-making.

Despite the hard work and extra hours, staff derive considerable pleasure from 'getting involved' with the making of films and always co-operate very willingly with these ventures and often offer their services as Extras.

The use of foreign locomotives is often necessary in the film making and being able to use engines and rolling stock from various parts of Europe in Britain has very obvious advantages. The location of the Nene Valley Railway enables London based companies to operate on a one-day visit if finances are tight.

With more recent additions to the filming list including James Bond in 'Goldeneye' and a two-part 'London's Burning' you no doubt will have seen the Nene Valley Railway many times to date. How many times have you seen it and not recognised the venue? The film makers craft often involves quite brilliant disguises.

BR 4-6-2 No. 70000 'Britannia' awaits departure from Platform 3 during the filming of the hit TV drama 'London's Burning'

Come and Join Us

Many visitors are surprised to learn that the Nene Valley Railway like most private steam railways is largely a volunteer organisation with only a very small proportion of paid staff. However, you don't have to be a working member to support the railway. Simply by becoming a member you give support and receive free *Nene Steam* magazines, can attend members' meetings and have concessionary travel.

But have you considered the advantages of active involvement? Working on the railway can be such a refreshing change from one's day-to-day work. Unwind from the hurly burly of everyday life by helping to run a friendly private railway. Jobs are available to meet all interests, ages and tastes, from engine driver to gardner. (Some jobs do, of course, require special training which you would receive as part of your promotion through the grades.

Volunteers are not expected to turn up every week, some appear once a month or less, while others come for their summer holidays. Remember it is possible to caravan in Ferry Meadows Park; Sacrewell Mill or Yarwell Mill and help on the railway at the same time!

As volunteers are the railway's single most valuable asset, they are encouraged to become involved in the running of the railway. The NVR is a democratic organisation and all members have a right to attend the Annual General Meeting and have their say.

The railway is heavily dependent on volunteer help. Will you join us?

Help is always needed and you are assured of a warm welcome. Please ask for a membership application form or write to:

The MEMBERSHIP SECRETARY
Nene Valley Railway,
Wansford Station, Stibbington,
PETERBOROUGH PE8 6LR

A busy scene at Wansford

9 780951 698068